I Am Who I Am

The Process

BENNY MARTINEZ

WESTBOW
PRESS®
A DIVISION OF THOMAS NELSON
& ZONDERVAN

WestBow Press books may be ordered through
booksellers or by contacting:

WestBow Press
A Division of Thomas Nelson & Zondervan
1663 Liberty Drive
Bloomington, IN 47403
www.westbowpress.com
1 (866) 928-1240

ISBN: 978-1-9736-6888-6 (sc)
ISBN: 978-1-9736-6890-9 (hc)
ISBN: 978-1-9736-6889-3 (e)

Library of Congress Control Number: 2019909260

Print information available on the last page.

WestBow Press rev. date: 10/16/2019

Foreword

Addiction. It is one of the most destructive conventions in the world today, crossing every continent, every border, every threshold in one way or another. When we are in the midst of it, we cannot see the destruction it creates. Yet even if we gain a glimpse of that destruction, we are powerless in ourselves to do anything about it.

But God...

Those two words change everything. In mercy, He reaches out to us, clearing away the lies that have blinded our minds in unbelief, and enabling us to respond to the truth of His love as exhibited 2,000 years ago on a brutal cross. Belief. Faith. That is all it takes, and yet that is the hardest step to make. Without the Holy Spirit enabling our minds to see, we would stay in the horror of addiction: addiction to pride, to drugs, to work, to technology, to alcohol, to self, to sin. We would never choose God. And even when God gives us understanding and calls us to Himself, He does not tap us with a magic wand and recreate us perfectly in the image of His Son Jesus Christ. No, He works on us gently, determinedly, persistently, consistently, just as a potter works on clay. Benny has started that journey that all Christ followers must take, and this book shares with you, the reader, the questions and struggles each of us undergo. It is indeed a journey, and Benny shares a raw, heartfelt glimpse into his life in a way that few are willing to do, exposing himself to inspection by those who may ridicule. Yet I believe that this book will strike a very real and raw nerve with all who have been on the receiving end of addiction, whether addicts themselves or family members. With a searing self-introspection, we may find more reality here and hopefully in ourselves than we imagined. I hope it speaks the truth of God's awesome work into your life, as He has worked in Benny's.

~~ Cindi Florit ~~

Dedication

This is dedicated to everyone who is fighting
the good fight to become more like Christ.
I wrote this for you. Keep going; He has
started a good work in you, and He will
carry it out until the day of completion.

Acknowledgements

I just want to say thank you to my mom and dad for always being in my corner and believing in me when no one else did. I want to thank my church, Faith Life in Port Charlotte, Fla., for showing me the love of God. Also thank you to all the people whom God has put in my life to show me His compassion and mercy. A special thanks goes to Cindi Florit for her encouragement and professional input into my manuscript.

About the Book

I subtitled this book of poetry "The Process" because most of the poems have to do with the shift from being utterly dead to being made vibrantly alive, the shift we all undergo when we decide to give our lives back to Whom they already belong — to Almighty God. I have been through some things I would much rather forget, and, thankfully, most of them are a distant memory and are fading the closer Christ draws me to Himself. I don't want you to look at me. I pray that you look at the pain and suffering I went through that He used to make me a better person for eternity in heaven with Him. That is my sincerest hope: that you will find solace in knowing the pain you are feeling is NOT meaningless. I would much rather that searching souls learn from my mistakes instead of learning them the hard way. Yet, learning them the hard way, as I have, makes their impact personal and lasting. You are not alone. There is Someone reaching for you, right at this moment. He is not here just to condemn you for your actions; He is here to tell you that you can be forgiven, and He longs for you to invite Him into your hearts, so He will then dwell within you and help you along this journey we call life. We were made to be the people we are, and not be the people this world is telling us to be. You are who you are, and I am who I am.

Adelyn's

My darling girl, I wish I could tell you I was a saint

But this is for you nonetheless, so you can see behind the paint

I just want to help you understand the hurt I put your mother through

That every time she had to make a decision, she was always thinking of you

Looking back, I don't comprehend my actions and all the pain I have caused

How I could so selfishly put you on the back burner and not think about the time I have lost

This is not me making excuses or placing the blame

Although I haven't been consistent, your mom has always been the same

She was there when I wasn't — I'm not going to lie anymore

The only thing I can tell you right now is I'll always be at the door

Maybe you won't open it when you know the full truth

But the only thing my heart is beating for right now is you

Some parents say they give life to their children, but in truth you gave me mine

You are the reason I got over myself,
the reason I walk that line

Anthem

I know Lord Christ is changing me; He is rearranging me

I'll scream from the rooftop He's saving me

This ain't an airport but it's plain to see

You think He saves His mercy, think He rations

You think people see God in the people you trashin'

You talk about doing drugs and expect no reaction

You know I got a drug, too, but mine's compassion

I can't change what I did; I can't change what I've done

But I'll tell you right now those days are done

It's a first for me, but this time I won't run

You think Jesus had that choice — the Lord's only begotten Son?

We walk around halfcocked saying that we tried

You think Jesus said that when He turned the tide

Were those His words when we pierced His side

People are scared to give it all because Him we crucified

Thank you, Lord, I'll praise You, Lord, till my throat is raw

And I know You catch me every time I fall

Go ahead make your excuses, run your jaw

Jesus, He gave us everything—why can't we all

This is not me downing or trying to criticize

But I, for one, am done with these self-serving lies

Because I know what I want destroys me; it's my demise

This is an anthem to get up
It's time to open your eyes

Apart

Not sure why, but my mind keeps pacing

Back and forth — don't know what I'm chasing

Words seem to flee my grasp

Unhinged, disconnected, unclasped

It seems I may have fit in

But that springs hope, so just kiddin'

But that need is oh-so real

In that area I can't change how I feel

That sense won't bend or break

Ignoring it is your first mistake

When you embrace what you can't hold

That's treatment for the soul

We all want to see, to believe

But in essence, that's how we're deceived

Some believe only what they hear

Most are trapped by what they fear

So, when seeing falls short of what you know

You can either believe the lies
or let faith grow

Armor of God

Coming out of it, you wonder how you ever went in

How you could turn your back on Someone so loving and sin again

How it was ever a choice, one only you could make

But at least now I know it's not me, but just a mistake

God will not condemn, that is written down in His Word

In the midst of it I prayed to You, and I know now You heard

I lost the battle but was rescued from the battlefield

So next time around I won't need to be, I have my protection of faith as my shield

As I sinned, I suffered as my flesh feasted on its destructive reward

But when the sin attacks again, I'll use His spirit as my sword

And as chaos consumed my muscle strands like a cannibalistic disease

Next time I'll remember to stand firm in my shoes made of peace

That instant when you feel dead inside, I know because I've felt it

But I know I have a Redeemer so his Salvation I put on as my helmet

So, when the world consumes you, just know you're not alone

He's calling you, my brother or sister in Christ
just pick up the ringing phone

Be Strong and Courageous

God says be strong and courageous; He is with us wherever we may go

And He gives us what we would ask for if we knew all there is to know

God is a beautiful orchestra; like Him they all work in tandem

And I refuse to believe these artificial trials happen at random

Your greatest weakness can be your mightiest strength, if you give it to our Father

There's not a single soul out there to whom He would say "why bother"

He loves us without partiality, and we all are made in His image

From murderers to the broken hearted, the boastful to the timid

We all are His children even though none of us can uphold His reputation

No matter how hard it is to see
we must find the I Am in every situation

Better Off

You say you can do better: well, here's your chance

I'd reminisce, but now I'm relieved this is our final dance

There's too much hurt to look past, and we've finally crossed that line

The only thing I need to focus on now is leaving you behind

I won't pretend I was a saint and that this is all your fault

But I also won't let you cauterize my wounds daily with your words made of salt

There's no sense in talking — you've said all you need to say

There's no sense of closure; I'll find that when I pray

I thought we would have something, a happily ever after

But the bad has shrouded the good, and all I can hear is your laughter

So, when the memories come in unannounced and make my perception soft

I'll remember your words to me
saying you're so much better off

Chained

I collapsed inside of Him, as I heard Him speak in the silence

He harbored me from my storm, He shielded me from the violence

And as I stared inside my head at the failures that condemn

He guided my sight through the night instead of dwelling on what could have been

I often overlook His unquestionable mercy

And now the only thing that keeps me going is I AM thinks I'm worthy

My mistakes — they claw at me with chains made of steel

They seek to imprison me
and deter me from following God's will.

Comfort Zone

I'm trying to let go of the things that used to be my home

But they fight back and chain me to my comfort zone

They want to confine me by thinking I am safe

But if I step back, I'll see that I'm just its slave

If I'm living in the little picture, then that's all I'll ever be

If I don't recognize the war that's raging, I'll lose my serenity

Distractions can keep us guessing what we are meant to build

And discouragement left to roam will cause us always to yield

But when we capture every thought that was meant to rob

And offer it to our Savior
I Am will do His job

Darkened Place

Do you feel that pulse in that somewhere deep inside

The growling of hunger as something is eating you alive

It has claws and teeth that are built to tear you to pieces

It has just one job, and it never slows or ceases

A million names and faces it's called and known by

It reminds you of every failure to convince you not to try

It can cause you to live in the agony of regret

Keeps you from nurturing a love that you haven't known yet

If it blinds you with its darkness, you don't know where to fight

And how can you hear I Am over your screaming in the night

If you're paralyzed in fear, playing dead is all you know

If you have no voice to stand on, then it will quickly take your soul

So, when it shakes you up at night, and you think hope is nowhere near

Stand firm and tell your demon
you will no longer live inside its fear

Dial Tone

I see a broken word on top a broken thing

That faithful dial tone, that familiar calling ring

And the gentle vibration seems to empty me

Of all discernment, of thinking coherently

It seems my mind it shutters, as if I've skipped a beat

I stand at my crossroads of where all my troubles meet

The one thing they have in common, the one consistency

Is that all my demons follow to wherever I may be

But now when they hunt me down, I don't rely on my own strength

I look to I AM, my Father
And His grace it never breaks

Elapsed

We can all look back at the time elapsed

Life and death, and how they overlap

We can watch a seed turn into a tree

But what can I do when you're wilting right in front of me

I reach out and try to nurture you, but I wasn't nurtured myself

How can I serve you while in identical shackles in a different cell

The selfish thing about it is that I try to help so I can feel better

And how can she trust me with all the hurt and lies I fed her

We think we reach a point when we think that we're alive

That we are just here to kill time and enjoy the wild ride

But it's simply not the case — we are here for a reason

We can ignore it or pursue it. Catch up, or it's leavin'

And I, for one, know how it feels to be left behind

> I'm still here -- I promise you
> but I'm trapped inside my mind

Escorted

I considered broken things as something to be ignored

Not knowing that they couldn't be — they were simply being stored

Not in a safe place, either, a place that breeds destruction

A place so deep inside you that can control your every function

It can use every breath you take as a weapon in its army

I have a first-hand account that evil has indeed scarred me

That evil was used as a catalyst for something else to follow through

I was escorted out of its clutches
so my testimony could help you

Fighting It

Dear Lord, You have awakened me, and now I'm declaring war

On the things that held me back from seeing what You have in store

I'm fighting myself boldly with every tooth and nail

And I know in You I will not falter. In the end, You will prevail

Your Word does not return void, and joyfully it has found me

Knowing now, looking back, it's always been around me

You have numbered my steps and given me a foundation

And now I'm fighting the things I used to be chasin'

I know You are good, and Your intentions are pure

You've hidden me as You worked on me, in Your love I was obscure

I am a misfit because this world has no claim on me

But there is work to be done, and I will do it patiently

There's a love in my heart for You, I'm no longer hiding it

You have begun a good work in me, and the darkness – I am fighting it

I'm fighting the thing I used to call my defender

But there's no address for him now, so I will return to sender

The dark things I ran toward instead of moving towards the Light

Are the things holding me back
But now I turn to fight

Finally

I'm starting to gather something that I've never really had

I've started focusing on the positive instead of holding in the bad

I can finally talk to my family, even look them in the eye

And know I'm finally not lying when I say I'll try

I can finally look at my mother and tell her she's been right all along

That You will always be there for Your children even when they are wrong

I can finally have a relationship without wondering what's the point

And finally take the consequences without a finger to point

I can finally be sober and still not look for a fix

And finally know in my heart
good and evil have no stable mix

Found

I don't need to be reminded of my past every single day

All I need is to trust in Your future because You are making a way

I've done things I'm not proud of, and that is the darkest part of my life

And every time I'm forced to remember, it cuts me like a knife

I'm trying to move on, slowly picking up the pieces

But my God's hand is over me, and it never slows or ceases

You are not a failure, you definitely had a rough start

But that beginning was a plan to discover who you are

And when you finally catch a glimpse of who He had in mind

You stop thinking you are the sheep that you thought He'd never find

The love of God can erase any debt because He knows the truth

That you are much more than your scars, and He gives the words to soothe

So, when you're lost in the wilderness of your past just know He's always around

<blockquote>
I was a lost, broken sheep
and at last, praise the Lord, I am found
</blockquote>

Grudges

Think about all your grudges and the grip that they hold

Forgiveness is the only love that can truly free the soul

But if you forgive, don't forget — we must learn from our mistakes

Ask God if it's worth it, and if it is, there's no chain He won't break

There's a million ways the devil can invade our minds

But there's a million-and-one-ways God won't leave us behind

He feeds the birds and clothes all the flowers

But aren't we more important? Through His grace He shows us His power

If you cannot forgive, then you won't be forgiven

And if you ask me
that's no way to be livin'

Half Measures

Half measures won't work if you want a place to stand

You see, when you give it all is when you fit into God's plan

The Lord won't take excuses because He already knows the results

But the Lord won't forsake you, either, for all of your many faults

If what you are thinking is positive, it originates from God

And if it makes you question your beliefs, it may be just a facade

The antithesis of God seeks to destroy

Controlling your mind, taking your joy

But we all have the weapon to win — it's God's Word

If you rebuke in His name, your faith will always be heard

Call out your demons, that's simply the only way

Because if you hide them, they will control you

So ask I Am
to take their power away

I Am Who I Am

I am who I am, and I'm not who I'm not

But if I'm going to give You me, expect my best shot

And if I fail, at least after that I would know

That if I ever tried to be You, then I would never grow

Seconds turn into minutes, minutes turn into hours

And no longer will I be the victim lost without power

I'm just trying to find out who I am, without what I'm expected to be

Through God I've found it, now with a crystal clarity

I've got myself a dark past, but in truth, who truly doesn't

I want to be the person God wants me to be, not someone who wasn't

I want to be the person who "did," not someone who "could of"

I want to do what He wants, not be someone who "should of"

All I can be is who I am, and all you can be is who you are

We have a lot of distance between us, but in the end it's not that far

Some look to this world, towards the shallowness and glory

But right now, I have my pen, so I'll write my own story

God already knows my outcome, and when and where I will breathe my last

But I can tell you it will not be breathed living in the past

There's a brighter future for us all, but we must reject the dark

The emptiness inside us can be scary, but there are no teeth with its bark

I am who I am, and that's all I could ever be

You are who you are, and only through your eyes you can see

Don't let other people make your choices because if you let them choose for you

When you see your purpose
from a different angle
it won't belong to you

I Forgive You

It has taken me so long to finally reach this stage

But I'm here now, and I'm so ready to turn the page

I held so much resentment, but I have no stones to throw

I've hurt just as much as I've been hurt, but now, I'm finally letting go

This hurts so much to write without pretending I'm the victim

You must forgive to be forgiven, in His Word that is written

I have forgiven all who've hurt me, now it's time to forgive myself

I forgive you for all you've done; it's time to step out of shame's cell

It's time to move on, time to put this all to rest

There's nothing holding you back now, no excuse to withhold your best

You have done some terrible things, and God has shown you mercy

So, who am I to keep it when His cup of wrath deferred ME

I'm sorry I forgot the love that our Savior has shown me

I'm sorry I gave up on you and treated you so coldly

The key to your chains and something I know is true

Is three redeeming words -- I forgive you

Forgiveness doesn't happen in an instant or a day

We all have run up a bill of sin that we could never pay

Sorries never spoken have a way to weigh you down

And forgiveness never given can kill your heart without a sound

If you won't allow healing, you can end up bitter and ashamed

When Jesus died upon that cross, love and anger were exchanged

Don't you get it? He paid the price for all of our transgressions

And now all He wants us to do is
follow that impression

I Hate You

I hate what I let you do to me on an everyday basis

Every time I'm hurt and angry, I turned to you to cover my bases

I'm sick of having no other resolve but to let you protect me

But the truth of it all is, you're only there to infect me

My pride, it covers me, and I refuse to let it go

Until it's much too late; then I'm left here all alone

I have this idea of what it should be, and when it doesn't measure up

I am left with all this anger, doomed to erupt

I thought I got you out, but in truth, I just dug you in

And who I'm talking to right now is my default nature in sin

I don't want to be who you want me to be — I've been there before

I keep asking myself the same question, "What do I invite you in for"

You are destroying my life until I'm stuck here with you

I second guess myself until it's literally all I can do

I'm so sick of you, but in truth, I'm just sick of myself

Why do I keep listening to your screaming, instead of asking for help?

You just want to destroy me, that's the only thing that gives you joy

Why do I keep letting you play with my life ever since I was a boy

Lord, help me, take control; I have no hands to steer

God, what good am I to You
if I'm isolated in his fear

I'm Selfish

I'm writing this because I need to know how I feel

There's so many voices talking, I don't know which to kill

Conflicting thoughts tackle each other, 'til I refuge in my box

All those rants and raves -- my own selfish paradox

I want to do the right thing, but then anger takes control

And it seems I'm thrown into the same fight I battled long ago

I want to say calming words that can ease and soothe your mind

But then selfishness sets in and again I'm steering blind

I want to feel your pain, but then I'm blindsided by my own

I want to hear your daily worries, but mine keep calling on the phone

I can tell you what's wrong with your life from the chair on which I sit

But all that leaves me being is a selfish hypocrite

I'm trying to walk with God, despite my shameful history

And now all I'm trying to do is follow Him consistently

But on the days I win, I fear the losing's close at hand

I'm trying to move on, but it feels like walking through the sand

Just when I start to lose hope, a new day has dawned

I can look back and see clearly all the people I have wronged

I want to encourage you, but then doubt discourages me

I start poking holes in your ambitions and sit back and watch you bleed

I don't know what is wrong with me, so I push your love away

Because all the jumbled thoughts I have leave me with no words left to say

I'm selfish -- that's the truth, but I can tell you I will fight

I don't want to be this way, like darkness must move from light

The Lord's Word resonated with me, which tells me I'm His child

But how long must a tiger be tamed before he forgets the wild

I'm not saying that I miss it because God knows that I don't

But how can I throw you a life preserver if I'm not even in the boat

This is my earnest prayer to You before I lose the ones I love

> Help me forsake my selfishness, I AM,
> please intervene from above

In the Middle

Good vs evil, on the right and on the left

But there's something in the middle Satan is aiming to ingest

He tries to take a bite every time we fail a test

He wants to cripple you, while God brings out your best

The one in the middle is you, and you decide who eats

One tries to elevate you, while the other offers only defeat

And if you choose the latter, you're doomed in the way it repeats

You can either be led into the light
or cover your tracks with deceit

Inspire or Entice

I'm here to tell you I've been broken, but I'm here to tell you I'm alive

What couldn't kill me makes me stronger, what didn't kill me makes me strive

We lose our focus when we struggle, but our focus is our will

You get to decide what you feed it; you get to decide where you kneel

We get to choose our chains by our choices — each one is a link

You can stand upon the Word of God or sit where you will sink

Our focus is our own, something our Father has freely given

We can either inspire or entice by our lives
and how we live 'em

Intentional God

My God is intentional

Not one dimensional

He paid the differential

Because He is the sentinel

He talks to us in our language, speaks in our tongue

He's the muscle that breathes life, the spiritual lung

He commandeers our restless souls when we invite Him in

He calls our very name, even though we are captivated in sin

He can break down any wall that we've built

He sifts us like gold from the never-ending silt

He procures us when we give Him our hearts

He can make any tortured soul
capable of a restart

Last Kiss

I still remember the last kiss that signaled farewell

The one, when remembered, still causes my heart to swell

The very kiss that dotted the last sentence of our final chapter

The final kiss I could agonizingly search for but know I'll never capture

The last time your lips touched my cheek, I felt your love breathe its last

And I so regretfully pushed it away -- then wanted it back so fast

I'll never forget you and the way I failed you completely

But I know we seek after the same God
so maybe there you'll finally meet me

Light

Sometimes I do feel broken, like I'm so terribly alone in the night

But I see You walking toward me; I can, because You are the light

And when Your hope illuminates all the shadows I've been fighting

None of them can measure up, and they disappear just like lightning

And as You walk towards me, I can feel You in my soul

With every step You come closer, the closer I am to being whole

You knew the only way to get through to me was beautiful persistence

I remember all You've done, so I stand and walk to close the distance

All the things that were holding me were slowly letting loose

Your love and mercy rescued me from the hangman's deadly noose

Darkness cannot move against You, not even the blackest night

You push back darkness wherever You go
because I Am is the light

Look at My Heart

Dear Lord, You have awakened a crippled, shattered thing

But Your strength and Your mercy allow my heart to sing

You have awakened something I didn't know was there

That hope so faithful that's cruel not to share

And You have loved me beautifully even before I knew my name

You know my every sin yet tell me not to be ashamed

Dear Lord, I thank You, humbly from the depths of my soul

You rescued me from darkness; You took back what the devil stole

Jesus, I am so thankful! Look at the intents of my heart

I Am burned my old away
which allowed me a beautiful restart

Love Your Neighbor

You got to love your neighbor, got to love the man inside the mirror

You got to love the ones who hurt you, the ones who made you live in fear

You've got to love the man beside, the one behind, just like the One above

Because I can promise you one thing -- there is nothing without love

I know it's hard, but forgiveness is the one and only key

From the prison your heart is in — please take that from me

You're holding onto grudges, but the truth is they are holding onto you

You need to forgive them, so God can finally forgive you

I'm not telling you it's simple, and that it happens overnight

But if you can't forgive them
your sins will never come to light

Making a Way

A broken thing inside a broken road

Never knowing which way I should go

So, I made a choice, and there I thought I stood

Making the decisions this world thought I should

But as time dragged on, so was I

Never knowing 'til awoken that I was living a lie

So, where I stood, that's where I fell

Trapped in my mind like a prison cell

I was looking for a way out, a way to escape

But my God Almighty's specialty is making a unique way

He made a path among the lies to follow

So, I took a step of faith, and my stupid pride I swallowed

But as I was walking, I noticed people still stuck in the trance

I tried to reach out, but they were
content in the world
and in its infinite dance

Mercy

Mercy is a word we've all heard but don't know the definition

It means not giving up on someone, and believing it's just a transition

Mercy is forgiveness when everything screams not to let it go

But mercy is how through us our Savior Himself can show

Mercy we've all been given and shown every second we're alive

Mercy is shown when we lose that battle we all wage inside

When the people you love break you, but you still believe in their soul

That is the love of Christ
that is not letting you let go

Merging

As our roads merge into union, we can walk a much straighter path

We can start seeing God as love and mercy instead of focusing on His wrath

When we let Him take control, He shows a freedom only He made and knows

And then we can march to the glory of God, instead of stepping on each other's toes

His love will never breed hatred, except the hatred of sin's chains

But He, too, will use them, like the sun uses many rains

He lets you see the darkness, so that you can see the stars

And sometimes you don't know freedom until you've been behind those bars

He shows contrasting paths and the outcome of them all

So, let the merging begin
when we surrender and answer His call

Middle Ground

What kind of thoughts do you empower?
Which ones do you take?

Do you live by your blessings?
Or remember the burdens of mistakes?

The mindset of a victim seems powerless and afraid
The prideful and arrogant think their lives -- **they**
have made

Do you let people walk across you as if you were a
ballroom floor?
Or do you have to elevate yourself by always having
more?

There's a middle ground I search for, but it seems a
constant battle
Ignoring my skeletons and the way their bones always
seem to rattle

They want your attention; without it they are nothing
but simple ghosts

They can make noise but can't truly hurt you as they
so arrogantly boast

The message I'm trying to convey — the truth that's in
these lines
That the middle ground between the two is where His
love resides

Stay away from pride, but have a rock on which you
stand

Remember we have a perpetual Creator
and you are just a mortal man

Move

It's been a while since I looked to You

But now I'm back again, broken, needing to know what to do

I need to look to You for answers because all of mine will lose

Dear Lord, one way or the other I just need You to move

My mistakes are catching up to me, and it is too much too bear

Even though I don't feel You, I know You're always there

You have been with me all my life—that's why I'm still alive

But I won't turn, I will wait for You — I'll be here when You arrive

I refuse to take another step until You tell me to go

Everything I thought I knew seems like it's dragging me in tow

"I have no idea what I'm doing" -- it's good to finally hear me say it

So, I look at my will, then my life, and at your feet I lay it

Do with it how You see fit, because I've had it my way

When I'm with You I can move, but without — I'm trapped inside the day

My pride is creeping back in, telling me to behave like a man

But it doesn't make any sense if I have no place to stand

I am so ungrateful when I don't remember what You did

Without You, I'm just selling my soul for the poorest highest bid

Please, Lord, I need You — You are the only One Who can soothe

So, let Your grace and mercy follow me
while I await for You to move

My Will

I remember when I was younger, I could always feel that infinite war

That constant push and pull of good and evil would always leave me torn

Both rational in their argument, or so I naively thought

And it was the louder of the two whose story I usually bought

One was screaming and clawing, the other stood firm and still

I didn't know I could speak up and choose who gets my will

I didn't know I played a role in this never-ending dance

But now that God has awakened me
I have a fighting chance

Needful Things

There're tales that don't need to be told

Lies priced and promised to be sold

There are things that lie dormant that should never be awoken

There is fire laced in gossip that is confidently spoken

The dead things we killed are screaming to be exhumed

There is pain cloaked in paranoia waiting the worst to be assumed

There's a hate that infests us if we leave it room to invade

Devils peddling their deceit for a price they say is easily paid

They use our wants and twist them until they're something we think we need

So, watch and beware the demons that trade God's truth and take the lead

Note to Self

This is a note to self, to the one who I thought who was protecting me

You were there when everyone laughed and started rejecting me

But all you did was tell me to hide, as you were neglecting me

Turns out, the truth of it all, is that YOU were infecting me

You were just trying to kill off only the best of me

And I've always been there as you stopped people walking all over me

And you kept me doped up on whatever was there, but I'm sorry this is the sober me

You had your time keeping me in the basement while you were acting soldierly

But hindsight is 20/20 now I can see that **you** were the one walking all over me

And you had me thinking that this was how it is, just the routine

As I am restless inside of my cell, I notice I'm the one who has been holding the keys

There's no sense in begging you let me out, as I've done a million times asking pretty please

All of the tears I've cried out, JUST LET ME OUT!!! Do you want me on my knees?

Through the window in that basement, I watched as you were destroying me

I don't need your permission, God told me to take back my life back, He showed me a vision

I see me smiling with no hurt in my eyes, my face without a disguise

I see my daughter when she is older, crying on my shoulder

AND THAT'S SOMETHING YOU'RE NOT GOING TO TAKE FROM ME!!!

If you think you are, you're thinking mistakenly

You've had enough of my life, you're not going to get anymore

You were the one holding me back, it's not going to happen no more

There's time to turn this around, without you thinking you're defending me

I don't need you, never did
God's protecting me

Paying the Bill

The deepest wound can carry a little scar

It can carry the pain of who you are

But it also can show your valleys that people question

How did you overcome it for us to mention

That question invokes an age-old need

Good vs evil and which does each choose to feed

You can deny His existence because He gave us free will

But then that leaves you in charge of paying the bill

God paid with sacrifice — He sent Christ so we could be free

Of the law Paul spoke of that wages in me

Potential

Right now, as you read this, I want you to wonder what you have

Not the things that could have been but right now and where you're at

And not the materialistic idols that this world holds so dear

Take a self-inventory of who you are, the time is now, place is here

What do you bring with you when you march from place to place?

And not your wallet or your credit cards, or the money in the bank

Not your belongings that can be taken with the simple act of theft

Mentally strip yourself down and take a tally of what's left

A concept many cannot grasp, without proof of their worth

And some simply will not do, without putting themselves first

But if you could, then how are you built — map out how you are wired

How many times can you pick yourself up before falling down tired

How many people can you save before you're in need of being saved

How many times can you be slighted before changing how you behave

How many times can you say something before your actions follow suit

> If you can do that right now
> then you've met the real you

Progress, Not Perfection

Progression in its defined state is a process towards a goal

Jesus is the example and the reason to be whole

But we will never reach that point on this earth because we made a choice

When we listened to our flesh and gave in to its seductive voice

Most of us feel broken because in a sense we assuredly are

We feel a disconnection when we don't embrace what we are

We are the hands and feet of our Creator — a great fact I do admire

And on that cross, He paid the cost for you and me as the Buyer

Progress not perfection — those words have instilled so much hope

Because you don't have to be perfect to believe and not just cope

I used to think to follow Jesus you had to look, to play the part

But I know now God loves you just the way you are

He loves you as much as He ever will — actions can't earn love

You are His sons and daughters that He made and watches from above

How we honor our Father is to show people what He's shown us

Ingrained in the mercy and grace He asks us to trust

I'm patient in this process not near perfect but still here

The more I trust in God the closer I get to changing gear

So, when people say I'm not good enough I can look at my reflection

And know what it's all about
is progress not perfection

Resetting the Soul

Praying is how we can reset the soul

Never giving up is how we can once again be whole

Giving it to God is how we replace what the devil stole

Because if we don't renew every morning the shame will take its toll

Crying is the canvas on which we express great grief

When broken beyond recognition is when we can finally find belief

And if you rebuke negative thoughts in Jesus' name, they must take their leave

Those thoughts are fiery darts the evil one merely uses to destroy and to deceive

So, when nothing is working, and you have nowhere to go

Invite faith in
to reset your wandering soul

Sand

Loneliness is something God gave us, as cruel as that may seem

He uses it to bring us closer, but we use it to the extreme

This day in age there're so many options for us to quench that thirst

But we forget the love that gave it to us to use on Him only first

If God is not an option, it can be used to self-destruct

And I have too picked a place upon its sand for a home I could construct

And when the waves came crashing in, that dwelling did collapse

Then left with the broken boards to build again from broken maps

I started to notice a pattern as my foundation kept eroding

I'd look upon the waves and see my broken shelter floating

I kept building things that were always destined to fall and fail

And I began to look at the home I built as just a prison cell

And when trapped inside yourself with loneliness as your one and only friend

You start to look for comfort in any way, any thing that you can

It can be sex, drugs, mutilation or whatever to help you stand

But your foundation will always crumble if it's built upon the sand

You don't know it's like a bandage on a bullet wound that will quickly fall away

And you'll have to use more of the same source to numb the pain away

So, when loneliness seeps in and tears you at your broken, tattered edge

Just know that a God so full of
love is reaching for you
as you stand upon that ledge

Scarecrow

With no power of your own, this world is a weapon

If you have no one to stand for, then what are you expectin'

When you have nothing, no hope but instant gratification

You live with the shame, like a shadow that never gives up chasin'

When you find another way through the one God appointed

You try to serve them both, but you always end up disappointed

You can't have more than one master because they lead to separate ways

One is elevation, the other is a perpetual maze

But when you stand with the Lord, the world as you know

Changes into what it actually is —
a faceless scarecrow

Shadow Boxing

When you're fighting your shadow, he knows your every move

He's your toughest opponent, and you're the one who always has to lose

Every time you throw a punch, he doesn't skip a beat

So, when you walk into that ring, that's the one you got to beat

But the ropes aren't where he's confined, he's ever present at the door

Every time you think you have an edge, he knocks you to the floor

The mirror speaks reflection, you determine what you see

The toughest person I'll ever fight
is staring back at me

Skeletons

When you know yourself utterly, it seems there's no escape.

From the skeletons in your closet that you think will keep you safe

The rattle of their bones keeps you restless all the night

Nothing can keep you from starved darkness but bringing them to light

We can hide our secrets, our sins, until we breathe our last

But you can never be alive in the present, if you don't forgive the past

We think that we hold grudges, but in truth our grudges hold onto us

They gorge on our identity, leaving nothing but the dust

Forgive and forget, a golden rule to be learned

Like you can't cross bridges you've already burned

We can make excuses, point fingers, live in fear

But the one who is always to blame
is the man inside the mirror

Sleeping

I am awake, but I was sleeping

Looking back, feels as if I was dreaming

I'm not so sure that my reflection speaks the truth

It's so confusing and bizarre caught up in your youth

You think you know everything, ironically you don't even know yourself

The accolades we accumulate collecting dust upon the shelf

We think they validate us, but in truth they only feed our pride

But true validation is knowing we have nothing left to hide

But as time elapses turning moments into years

God slowly refines you
as you overcome your fears

Taylor

I'd just like to take a moment and turn my focus to you

A sigh of relief comes out of me every time that I do

We've been through hades and back, baby; only you and
I understand

We walked into each other's lives but it's almost like we ran

I saw a beautiful girl who was trapped inside her pain

So how is she my rainbow that's always following the rain

Baby, you are so strong and stubborn to your core

And when I see you, I'm adrift and start swimming to
your shore

There're so many "sorries" I want to say, but don't want
to reopen old wounds

But they were actions of an addict
and thankfully now I'm addicted to you

Thank You

I just want to say thank You because I know I don't say it nearly enough

I just want to say thank You for all the things I wanted and You kept me out of because of Your love

Thank You for all the times You told me no because You know what I want destroys me

Thank You for breaking me down to silence so I could hear You because it was too noisy

I just want to hear You, and every direction You tell me to take

Because when I follow You, I know I'm not a mistake

I know I can be something, but I need You to tell me what it could be

> Without I Am I'm nothing —
> I was blind but now I can see

This, Too, Shall Pass

They say every storm will run out of the rain

And in this world, there's necessary refining pain

Although as you walk it's sometimes all you feel

But behind the scenes you know you're learning to heal

You can evolve into things you never knew existed

In the index of life, these things were never listed

So, when you become something that you hate

Just know it doesn't have to be
your dying fate.

Time to Pray

Time to pray. You think I'm talking about later, no, now

Repeat after me: He will hear you out

Lord, I give you the reins of every second of every day

Lord, take the wheel, let Your Holy Spirit pray

Tell Him you're done with your own strength and you know He's the way

Mean this with heart, say amen, in the name of Jesus you pray

You feel the goosebumps and the chill down your spine

That's Him and His love — His most precious design

Jesus healed the sick, gave sight to the blind

There's not a single person in this room He wants to leave behind

But it's time to get up like He told Joseph in the middle of the night

He's trying to save you, trying to bring you towards the light

If you ask me, that's something so amazing

Forget about these lines and the words I'm phrasing

This world is dark and so are the things we're chasing

There's only One Thing so beautiful
that we need to be praising

Tit for Tat

We've all dealt a hand in this never-ending game

The savagery of hurting someone because you know they'd do the same

They say an eye for an eye, a tooth for a tooth

Just leaves you looking for a fight, in need of an excuse

Two wrongs never make a right, and that's how it will always be

And every time I point a finger, there're three pointing back at me

You hurt me, I hurt you worse, a perpetual cycle

Can turn the one you love the most into your most vicious rival

I'm caught up in this game and the only way to ever break it

Is the next time you get hit, lay down your weapon and take it

It will feel like you're being walked on, but no, that's just your pride

That's the thing that holds you captive
while it's eating you alive

Unanimous Tears

There're tears you have to cry no matter how much you push and pull

The art of grieving to help move on that God has given us as a tool

Our way of expressing loss is unique to us in our own way

But tears are unanimous in the sense that shedding them is how we pay

And if you let them build up, you can drown in your sleep

But water is how the seed we sew grows so ready to reap

So, if you're wondering, like I did, why your life is so dry

It's that the only way life's rivers will run is
if you're courageous enough to cry

Us

In life there's a winner and a loser

There's the used and the user

A simple truth you can't evade

We all have to lie in the bed we've made

A rigid pattern that we're doomed to repeat

Live in the consequences of our own deceit

No patience — we want instant gratification

Sell our souls for our fix with no hesitation

Our morals right and wrong, being tossed to the wind

For the supplication of self-centeredness, with no end

They say put yourselves first, and you'll be rewarded

But your soul is the price
for all you've afforded

83

The Walking Dead

Something that still moves but you see no life in their eyes

Has been tricked, promised to the world, with no hope in all their lies

They move from place to place with no real sense of direction

Picked apart so many times, like a corpse in need of dissection

You can feel a sense of numb when they look you in the eye

Like a bird with clipped feathers with no ability to fly

They smile with their teeth; all you see are jagged tips

They can freeze you to your core, with words falling from their lips

The ones they have in the movies have it wrong in the end

They are not looking to devour you, but something's eating them

Some wear pain with content because that's all they ever know

Others live inside their past, incapable of letting go

So, if at any point you wonder where have I been led

Pray to God to save your soul
from being the walking dead

Waxing and Waning

❧ ❧

I look up at the night sky, and admire God's creation of the moon

It's always in transition, from full to nothing so soon

Something I can relate to, kind of like looking at my mirror image

It's always waxing and waning in an endless dance of scrimmage

Sometimes I can see where my feet fall from its light cast by the sun

But sometimes it's so pitch black it feels like the light has been overrun

Just when you think you know what to expect, a sliver starts to shine

You can see it come to life, as how it is defined

When light enters the picture, nothing can stay the same

When it starts to emerge, everything is being driven outside the frame

And the moon reflects that battle, a scene played every night

The light can leave somebody, but it always returns to fight

Darkness is always present; it is the easiest route

But when light starts moving in, emptiness is on its way out

Next time you look at the moon, and you notice it's going dim

Just know the light will return to fight
and win the battle again

We Miss You

Please don't take this as me judging, because I've been through it before

I can now see what I did to my family, how I hurt them to their core

In my head I thought I was worthless, and my actions couldn't affect another

But all that changed when I heard I was a lost soul to my own mother

I didn't blame her, I just took a moment to reflect

Honestly looking at myself in the way you would dissect

Something got strong in me and my excuses weren't holding up

Finally, I could see how selfish it is to be content in not getting back up

When you choose a life of drugs, you're abandoning who you are

Leaving all the people who love you wishing on a star

I'm telling you it's not too late; it's time to open your eyes

You don't want to stay where you're at strung up in all the lies

There's a better life for you, if you want it; you just have to leave the poison right here

I know you're scared — so was I — but doing drugs is how we live inside our fear

It'll be worth it, I promise; you just need a little hope

Focus on the good instead of finding reasons why to cope

Life can be beautiful, but you don't notice it when wrapped in chains

Do you want something controlling you, keeping you from changing lanes

We miss you and you can do this, please just leave it all behind

The only thing it does for you is slowly turn you blind

Maybe not your sight but blind to everything's beauty

Please listen to their love through this poem
their hearts speak through me

We Will See

What's another hurt? Just figure out a way to carry it

Or put it with the others and just go ahead and bury it

But which will be the straw that breaks the camel's back

How far can you go before there is no turning back

How do you know when you've had enough

When do we stop calling each other's bluff

Confused and broken can be misunderstood

So can the weakness of not standing when you should

So, when you're on the edge of falling apart

There's got to be something to awaken your heart

You might have to push and pull but you can always find it

And whatever it is, hold it and stand behind it

If it's worth it, we will see there's no need to fight

Just know that I love you
so let's just rest easy tonight

When You Know

There was a time, maybe short, maybe small

That our hearts were not receptive to His call

But His mercy was patient and kind

He's the God Who gave sight to the blind

He is here on every level of all stages

We might be in our own stories, but He wrote all the pages

We all have things that at a time we once knew

But believe Him when He says all the things have become new

I am not perfect, and I will never claim to be

But I can tell you one thing — His Holy Spirit is working in me

He took us all out of bondage — we must never forget

How He gave His only Son to pay our enormous debt

When you know you have changed because of His grace

There is not a thing in this world
that can take His place

Who You Are

You cannot find out who you are if you're locked inside a box

'Who you are" to me is how I am unorthodox

Because if we've all walked the same pattern, how would we know there's another way

Like somethings do not change — like the darkest hours come first in each and every day

"Who you are" to me is who I am alone

"Who you are" to me is how you act at home

It's the face you have on, the one you see inside the mirror

Or could it be a charade in terms of living in constant fear

What do you really want to say, and how do you really want to speak it

Do you want to be suppressed inside that box before you ever seek it

What you do is not who you are, it's before you were ever on the clock

What did your actions really prove — how were they taken stock

If it all ended today, how would you feel looking back

Because who you are might be how you feel after the final act

When finally examined by our Maker, what will be our final grade

> Who you are to me is where you end
> they are the paths that you've made

Why?

Why is this so hard, why am I so confused

At the end of every day, why do I feel so unused

I don't know how to turn to You when self-destruction is all I've ever known

How do I forget this hurt when I'm always sitting here alone

I don't know Your plan, and what this day is supposed to bring

But I still look to you, Lord, and one day I want to sing

I don't know what else to say that I haven't already said

I feel like a decorated Christmas tree counting the seconds till I'm dead

I feel like there is more to me, but I haven't quite yet tapped

Lord, I'm asking this question to You
why do I feel so trapped

You Do

Dear Lord, we are broken; you can see that from Your throne

You can see our scars, all our broken hearts, the shame in every bone

Though we are changing, we know that for all time — You are the same

You know the intentions of all our hearts, You know us by our very names

You bring us to our knees with the depth of Your mercy

And when I feel that in my heart, that love I am so unworthy

You pour out Your grace so freely from heaven's gates above

And You love everyone as if they were the only one to love

I know You send Your blessings that don't fit into our plans

But Your ways aren't our ways, and now we have a better place to stand

You equip us with what we need through each and every season

And my soul has been searching for You
since I was old enough to reason

Index

These are the reasons why I wrote these poems. They will mean different things to you because we are not the same person, but I want to clear up any confusion I may have caused

Adelyn's— This is to my daughter and her mother finally owning up to all of my mistakes

Anthem— I wrote this in kind of a rapping format, a dedication to all the work God has put into me and hopefully to instill hope into you

Apart— The feeling of hope when you had none before, struggling with putting it into actions and letting your faith grow

Armor of God— I was reading the Bible one night and came across Ephesians 6:11. I started writing this to show you how I applied this Bible passage to my life and maybe how to apply it to yours

Be Strong and Courageous- These are the words God spoke to Moses to tell Joshua when they were finally going into the Promised Land. These are the words He is telling us now, too

Better Off- I wrote this because there are people who are going to say they are better off without you, but maybe you both are better off without each other

Chained- This was to shed light on the chains this world can confine you with and to know that God is your harbor from them

Comfort Zone- This poem describes coming out of your comfort zone. Though your comfort zone is different than mine, God will always call you out of it to find His purpose for your life

Darkened Place- I wrote this going through a difficult time in my life. God had started to make me aware of my inner demons. He was showing me that we all have them, and we must not listen to them. If the devil is talking, he is lying

Dial Tone- This was to manifest the triggers we all have to certain unhealthy, ungodly things. If you don't know something is there, you can't fight it

Elapsed- This entry was to convey a sense of time passing without my even knowing it. A feeling of watching someone you love deteriorate right in front of your eyes and feeling helpless to do anything about it

Escorted– This is to people (like me) who try to bury things inside ourselves and why it can be dangerous to do so

Fighting It– This is among a few in here that I wrote to declare war on myself, to fight all of the things that I have allowed to take root in me. This poem was important to me because I was actually starting to see the progress God has been making in my mind

Finally– This poem speaks of progress in your life and in mine — the feeling of finally being able to do something genuine

Found– This one speaks to the joy of finally coming to a path that leads me where God wants me to go

Grudges– Grudges speaks to the stronghold in our minds. We must forgive to be forgiven. The enemy finds sure footing in unforgiveness

Half Measures– In the Word, numerous times it refers to "all your heart and soul" — it doesn't allow half measures

I Am Who I Am– This was the final poem I wrote for this book. Simply put, God made you to be you. So be who God has called you to be, not what this world wants you to be

I Forgive You– There is a very strong case in the Word for forgiveness, but along with other people you must forgive yourself. God will if you ask Him to with a humble heart

I Hate You– The strongest motivation to change is not love; it is hate. When you finally start hating the default setting of sin in your heart and mind, you can begin to overcome it

I'm Selfish– I wrote this to forsake the selfishness in my heart. It was painful to write, but I did it because we all can be selfish sometimes, and God will help you if you ask Him

In the Middle– I have always been keen to the cartoons of the angel on one shoulder and the demon on the other. What I thought wasn't given justice was the person in the middle — he decides who eats. If you feed your faith, your doubts will starve to death

Inspire or Entice– We all have a decision to make for other people to see

Intentional God– Our Father does not make mistakes. He will not stop until His vines are producing the fruits He intends for them to produce

Last Kiss– I wrote this after pushing away the love of someone who means so much to me

Light– Nothing can stand in our Father's light without being changed. And if it doesn't want to change, it flees

Look at My Heart– I remember writing this and being so thankful that even if I was in the wrong place at the wrong time, He could still see my heart wasn't

Love Your Neighbor- God demonstrated His love for us when He sent His Son to pay for mankind's sins. He made us in His image, so I am led to believe we must show our love because that's what He has shown us. The parable of the servant who owed much who would not forgive another who owed little is the basis

Making a Way- God has and always will be the God of making a way. Some do not want His ways and it's sad, but He will make a way

Mercy- I wrote this for a better understanding of the definition. I wanted to understand what it means so I could stop taking it for granted

Merging- This poem was to portray the path to becoming more like Christ

Middle Ground- This entry, to me, speaks to the place I've longed for between arrogance and timidity — the place where love resides

Move- We have hills and valleys in our lives, and sometimes when we are going through a valley, we just need to wait for God to move

My Will- What we choose to focus on is our freewill, we get to decide

Needful Things- There's things that we want, and the enemy will twist them until it's something we think we need

Note to Self- This poem helped me understand the war going on in my head. I used to choose the voice that told me to be selfish.

Then I started to choose the still, small voice and declared war on the other

Paying the Bill- Jesus already paid sin's debt. He was and is the perfect sacrifice to atone for the great debt of sin in all of our lives

Potential- Sometimes we mistake money and power for worth. Jesus didn't need money, and He is power but never used it for His own sake as a man. This poem is to make people dig a little deeper in themselves and find their true potential

Progress, Not Perfection- I wrote this to help who ever reads it know that God doesn't expect perfection out of us. He just wants us to keep getting back up and keep going

Resetting the Soul- I wrote this to express how much we all need a restart, and if you ask God, He will give you one

Sand- This poem speaks to each and every one of us. At some point in our lives we have all tried to build things on sand

Scarecrow- This poem was to shed light on trying to serve more than one master

Shadow Boxing- "Get out of your own way." I've had so many people tell me that, and I wanted to know what it means so I wrote this poem. You have to fight the old you for space so the new you can move in

Skeletons– We have to confront the ghosts of the past to move on. We can't be alive in the present if we don't forgive the past

Sleeping– This signifies finally waking up and looking back at everything with a different point of view

Taylor– I wrote this to my soon-to-be wife. I dragged her through anguish and did unspeakable things to her, but she stood by me through all of it. This is dedicated to the love of my life. Thank you, Taylor, for never giving up on me

Thank you– This is a poem of gratitude to the Lord. He is the way, truth, life and our light

This, Too, Shall Pass– This poem is to people trapped in this world and not wanting to be there — people who have come to hate themselves like I did

Time to Pray– I wrote this kind of like a salvation prayer. I want people to pray this to God and invite Him in. He will show up. The reference to Joseph is when God told him in a dream to take Mary and Jesus to Egypt

Tit for Tat– This entry deals with repaying evil for evil

Unanimous Tears– I firmly believe that there are tears that we have to shed to finally be reset

Us– Speaks to giving up the life God has for you for something that destroys you

The Walking Dead- We have all come across people who are lost and have given up on themselves. I pray this poem can relate to them and give them hope.

Waxing and Waning- The moon changes every night, and so do we. It illustrates the change in us

We Miss You- I wrote this poem from the point of view of someone who has gone through drug addiction. I had a couple people in mind when writing this, the closest to me — my brother. We miss you, Josh

We Will See- I wrote this one to people going through rough patches with their spouse. Only time will tell what's going to happen

When You Know- This poem is for people who know that the Lord our God brought us out of bondage and is working in us

Who You Are- What this world has made you believe about yourself is not who you are. God knows exactly who you are. It's not how you start things — it's how you finish them

Why? - A poem of lament. A prayer of questions that He is answering every day I'm alive

You Do- I asked myself a question a while back, "Who can see me?" And my answer was: You do